Simone Awoke!

A Division of The McGraw·Hill Companies

Columbus, Ohio

www.sra4kids.com

SRA/McGraw-Hill
*A Division of The **McGraw·Hill** Companies*

Copyright © 2002 by SRA/McGraw-Hill.

All rights reserved. Except as permitted under the United States Copyright Act, no part of this publication may be reproduced or distributed in any form or by any means, or stored in a database or retrieval system, without prior written permission from the publisher.

Printed in the United States of America.

Send all inquiries to:
SRA/McGraw-Hill
8787 Orion Place
Columbus, OH 43240-4027

ISBN 0-07-569729-7
 2 3 4 5 6 7 8 9 DBH 05 04 03 02

The alarm awoke Simone.

Simone slid down the pole.

Simone's role was no joke.

Simone rode to the fire.
She hoped she was not too late.

Simone noted the smoke.

Then the alarm awoke Simone!